THE WIND OF OUR GOING

Books by Patricia Goedicke

THE WIND
OF OUR GOING

POEMS BY

Patricia Goedicke

COPPER CANYON PRESS · PORT TOWNSEND · 1985

GRATEFUL ACKNOWLEDGMENT IS MADE TO THE FOLLOWING
PERIODICALS IN WHICH SOME OF THESE POEMS FIRST APPEARED:

American Poetry Review ("Hands That Have Waved Farewell,"
"Whether a Bright Stranger"), *Another Chicago Magazine* ("In
the Lap of the Body," "The Bus at Midnight"), *The Chariton
Review, The Chowder Review, Cutbank, Hampden-Sydney
Poetry Review, The Hudson Review* ("Full Circle"), The Kansas
Quarterly ("The Interior Music"), *The Massachusetts Review,
The New England Review, New Letters, The New Yorker* ("In
the Aquarium," "Mahler in the Living Room," "The Reading
Club"), *Northwest Review, Ploughshares, Poetry East* ("The
Entire Catch"), *Poetry Northwest, The Slackwater Review,
Stone Country, Studia Mystica, Tendril, Three Rivers Poetry
Journal* ("The Husband and Wife Team").

THE PUBLICATION OF THIS BOOK IS MADE POSSIBLE BY A GRANT
FROM THE NATIONAL ENDOWMENT FOR THE ARTS.
COPPER CANYON PRESS IS IN RESIDENCE WITH CENTRUM AT
FORT WORDEN STATE PARK.

ISBN 0-914742-84-1
LIBRARY OF CONGRESS CATALOG CARD NUMBER : 84-73336

COPPER CANYON PRESS
POST OFFICE BOX 271
PORT TOWNSEND, WASHINGTON 98368

CONTENTS

Prelude

I. The Real Story

II. This Moment

III. Entering the Garden

FOR MY SISTER

JEAN-MARIE McKENNA COOK

O my friends why are we so weak
In winter sunlight why do our knees knock,
Why do we walk with small steps, ugly
And spindly as baby birds

Whose world do we think this is?
O my friends take it,
O my friends don't look at each other
Or anyone else before you speak.

I have had enough of scared field mice
With trembling pink ears,
I have had enough of damp
Diffident handshakes,

Do you think I haven't been stepped on by giants?
Do you think my teachers didn't stand me in a corner
For breathing, do you think my own father didn't burn me
With the wrath of a blast furnace for wanting to sit on his knee?

Indeed I have been pressed between steamrollers,
I have had both my feet cut off, and the pancreas
And the liver and the lungs of the one I love
Have been sucked out of my life and the air around me

Has turned to cereal, how will I stand up,
What opinions can I offer but I will not be silent,
There are dogs who keep their skinny tails
Permanently between their legs

But also there are sleek horses, as easily as there are curs
There are squash blossoms that flower around fountains
Like white butterflies, there is courage everywhere,
For every reluctant nail-biter

There are a hundred raised fists, for every broken broomstick
There are millions of bent grasses snapping
Back and forth at the sky, beating the blue carpet
As hard as they can, with the frail tassels of their hair

For every pair of eyes squeezed tight
Under colorless lids there are thousands of others
Wide-open, on the proud columns of their necks turning,
Observing everything like King Radar,

O my friends for all the sad rain in heaven
Filling our dinner plates you have ten fingers of honey
Which are your own, stretch them, stick them up
And then wave to me, put your arms around each other's shoulders

When we meet in a field with no fences
The horizon is yours, and the books and all the opinions
And the water which is wine and the best bed
You can possibly think of to lie in.

I.

THE REAL STORY

MAHLER IN THE LIVING ROOM

Low to the ground, the windows are full of lake water.
Leaden, the pure slabs rise straight up into the air

From the summerhouse, where we sit watching them,
Shivering on the threshold of late fall

As the bronze hills in their shabby coats
Arch themselves like hands over a cold radiator —

And Mahler in the living room like an earthquake. Behind the eyes
Sorrow heaves upward, the heavy planks of it gigantic

As armies at a distance, as oak trees, as the tar surface
Of a road giving way to frost, buckling under and over

To the white forces of winter: the underground tears bent
Like ribs cracking, hundreds of paralyzed veins

That are now, suddenly, released, in great silver floods
Powerful as oceans our whole lives rise up

Into a sky full of planets tumbling and shooting,
First lavender, then apricot, then plum-colored:

Hissing like skyrockets they streak
Over the slumberous oars in the depths voluptuously rowing

Velvet as elephants, whose liquid footsteps wallow
About to submerge everything: dock, landing place, lawn...

But there are jagged slashes, too,
Impertinent brass flourishes, horns that bite air

And bray at each other like gold rifles

Over the little pebbles, the quaint Chinese sparrows
Of the piccolos humorously yammering, trying not to listen

To the huge hesitation waltz beneath them,
The passionate kettledrums rolling

In the throbbing cradle of the gut
Sighing over and over Let Go,

Abandon yourself to the pain, the wild love of it that surges,
Resistless, through everyone's secret bowels

Till the walls almost collapse, our clothes fall from us like leaves
Trembling, helplessly tossed

In an uncontrollable windstorm, the branches weave and sob
As is if they would never stop, unbearable the sky,

Unbearable the weight of it, the loss, solitude, suffering,
The hills staring at us blindly,

The house nothing but a shell, the bare floors
Relentless, our eyes welling over with such pain

It is all absolutely uncontainable, in a few minutes
Surely everything will dissolve...

When the first duck of a new movement appears

In the middle distance, the bottlegreen oboe bobs
Blue-ringed, graceful, under the little rowboat;

The invisible red feet sturdily paddle
Like webbed spoons in the chill soup of the water

That turns into a flatness now,
The agonized surface lies down

In the glass eyes of the windows,
Those solid transparencies

We orchestrate ourselves
To keep the world framed, at bay

As the great lake of the symphony sways
Far down, far down

The violent sun sets,
Over the wet shingles, the shining flanks of the house

The threadbare arm of the hills sinks,
The wave of feeling rests.

On the falling elevator trapped as the sixty-one floors blink
Like eyes in sequence, each possible resting place whipping by

Faster and faster, one after the other, Hello
Goodbye, my friends, yesterday we were talking, today we die

In our sleep, with the stars falling, surely it is the stars
In waterfalls of sparks, ribbons of light descending

With tennis racquets, Bibles, cars, violets, young men wearing hats
Ski lifts in winter, *The New York Times*, the Funnies,

All the intense conversations that will never end,
Your photograph on my wall, mine tucked in your billfold,

Do you know what you look like? Not now you don't,
Maybe one second ago you did, but the bits and pieces of yesterday

Are piling up, pushing (some even going on ahead),
There's Mother, there's Father, there's Edward from the first grade

And Beethoven's Ninth, and the Bach B Minor, each chord
Turns into a glissando, clusters of fireworks flying

With curses, cats wailing, the whine of the big guns
And desperate bombs going off, the little pot bellies

Of starved children, presidents, old beggars, vice-presidents,
Every newspaper headline, every last quarrel

We ever had, each hangover, each miraculous glass
Of the deep bourbon of love, even the pure silence of prayer

Is pouring past us like rain, like a blizzard of hard rice
Sliding by, sliding by, polished smooth as the ground

Each of us thinks he is standing on, certainly I do
Content, watching the world go by but suddenly

The bottom drops out, the stomach crazily catapults
Past the toes, the feet, the head follows, mountains

Exchange places with the back yard, even your face
Revolves in the sky, it's the Big Dipper, upside down

The wind roars in our ears, in the dizzy whirl of the blood
There's no turning back, on parallel tracks shooting

From the cliff of our birth we keep falling,
First you, then me, then me rushing by you.

IN THE AQUARIUM

From the front door to the back garden
The guests stream through the house in a straight line

And then stop, milling around on the windy lawn
Like dark fish in an aquarium

Restlessly, under the night sky,
The moon like a superior ship driving us

Just short of the small, protectively calm pool
We have formed around our blind friend

Who is backed up against the wall in a thick sweater
Clumsily buttoned over one breast,

While cold fingers the naked arms
Of the rest of us, shifting our feet

Like blinkered horses at the curb, we nod
And concentrate on each other uneasily,

From time to time twitching our skins
Under the trees waving like seaweed

Under the open eye of a moon
Our blind friend cannot see but must feel—

Cloudy illuminations like a hand stirring the water,
Our jeweled scales, our neat tails shifting

In and out of the shadows swimming
Below the second-floor windows, in the lamplight,

Where, suddenly, I notice,
Like a fist looming against glass,

The sinister bulk shape of someone watching us
So secretly I begin to shiver;

Under that arrogrant gaze
Guiltily I go on watching our blind friend

And being watched myself,
Like drowned sailors we are all of us unaware

Of anything more than a few of the undercurrents
Drifting through the bowl of evening;

So many alien stars, red coral reefs growing
From the glass floor of the garden,

Drinks flashing, one or two watchdogs, cats
With their strange fixed stare.

THE BUS AT MIDNIGHT

The bus grunts,
Tries to turn into the wrong street.

Out of the underwaters of sleep
I leap up suddenly, I run to the window

And there it is, like a nuclear submarine or a palace,
Strange UFO of the deep.

Having deserted its regular route like a bandit

Majestic as three or four elephants linked together
With amber backup lights glowing, the eyes

Of a huge snowplow sweeping across white sheets,

Over these narrow cobblestones it is a whale
At midnight, groaning and thrashing

On a dry beach.

With one red eye and one green eye
Stuck out like a lobster's directional lollipops

It grinds gears, it lurches
From one side of the sharp corner to the other

Like an old wino, a prehistoric grouper

On its hind legs it is a grizzly
Flexing its arms, and threatening

To ravish our thin tent,

I know it in my stomach, I remember
The night of the air raid siren

Across the street, in the park
The night of the crooked cops

And I am afraid, has it come for me at last?
Packed tight with people

But still questing everywhere, a boa constrictor

Even though it is clearly mistaken,
Stupid as a stuffed codpiece

It keeps right on coming,
Pushing and pulling at the house

More powerfully than Zeus's swan
Implacably it appears to me, transfixed

Unable to move, quivering
Like a school of minnows I stare

At this awkward rhinoceros, bull-necked
Red-nosed comedian of the Absurd...

If only I could wake you!
But even you couldn't stop it,

If all the passengers are trapped
Inside their own terror, stunned

By the trick eel of Accident

All we can do is wait:
If this be a Messenger I pray

This bus like a wild boar,
This bus like the end of the world,

This bus like a blind phallus
Is knocking at the wrong door.

The faces of some houses stand up like tombstones
Especially in New England, rigid among granite hills,
Almost disdainfully the bleak windows stare
Neither out nor in. Spare, glimmering, quiet
They simply refuse to speak to us: words chiseled into their sides
Have nothing but facts to say, they lean back from the roads
Stiffly, whether they have been dressed up
Or down, whether their clapboards shine like policemen's bridles
Or sink in exhausted heaps to the bare ground.

Trying to decipher them, the illegible scribbles of their gutters
We see them in our dreams making pronouncements
We do not understand. They are distant, cold,
Forlorn. Who lives in them? Sometimes the fat cars
Of Calvinist popes slide down the driveways
Bearing businessmen and mink coats, sometimes rifles
And sometimes even typewriters, to the ruling whisper of dollars
Rustling behind blinds, the clink of steel muttering
Unintelligibly through the crisscross bars of our minds.

But the litter around some of them, woolen wigs on the ground,
Ripped pillow cases, law books, frayed hair ribbons dangling,
Bicycle pumps, pigs rooting, water-logged sofas remind us
Of beggars beside the Ganges, old women in Mexico
Selling handfuls of seed in the open doorways of hovels
Not much dirtier than these, with the gap teeth of nightmare
Poking their fingers at us, in the glare of glass
Silent as bone, the lidless eyes of school teachers
Rattling their papers at us and then going home

To strange living rooms, lives we never knew
And why should we? We would peel off each shingle to find out
Behind their faces what they did with their judgments of us:
Were we good? Bad? We keep wondering and wondering,
But those long ago verdicts have nothing to do with now,
Probably they'd never even remember us,

The houses pull their front lawns up to their doors
While we cower before them, exaggerating our terror
Of anonymous Forces, mysterious Great Powers

We invented ourselves, in a glut of pure masochism,
Guilt wallowing in the cars of political systems
That are always there to be blamed, behind every facade
Miss Granville raps her desk, she shakes her head and frowns
But no, it is only the blue flare of television
Lighting up one of the windows, if only we could accept it
However painfully, the one thing we refuse to feel
In public, though inside everyone it is the same,
Over all the rationalizations falling like poisonous rain

And no judgment can appeal it. The dream trial goes on
Implacably, the prosecutor hints there is something more,
Something we have forgotten, and suddenly I remember Nicholas
In full sunlight, strapped to his wheelchair again,
White-faced but determined, awkward spectacles glittering at us
At the end of his young life as frail, picky, intelligent
As we were stupidly fearful, knowing he was going to die
We kept turning away from him, however long he waited for us
With what neutral sweetness, to look him in the eye.

FULL CIRCLE

1.

Next door it has been quiet
Almost a year   since she vanished

Into the meatgrinder   cells
Monstrously exploding   gone

But still we hear her   sometimes
On the other side of the wall

The hoarse voice calls our names

As it often did, toward the end
Approaching as she disappeared

She swore she would come back,

But sitting in the weak sun
Defiant, painting her toenails red she'd relax

Only a few minutes,
Then get up and roar off

In her high-powered car to telephone a lover
Or check up on a friend   or her two sons,

She said she wanted to trust us

But jaunty in her slim blue jeans,
Brief ponytail wagging

When we went out to eat together
She always paid for herself,

She'd stiffen against us, insisting
We were to be taken care of   first

But with what delicacy in her shoulders
And what humor in her wrists!

Casual as chrysanthemums
Spicy, lining fall borders

In her flaming extremities what contempt
For the white gloves of a past

She still drank, still chain-smoked bitterly
On runaway grown-up feet to avoid,

For she was a lion of great power:

Because she had deserted them   once
She wrote to her parents faithfully

Crossed oceans to visit

But even in the middle of a smile
Her friends had learned, long since

To be careful of it, the sudden
Fierce show of white teeth

For she was afraid of us   also
Stupidly we did not know

Out of our own terminal ache

We kept trying to protect her,
Kept trying to turn her

Into an equal   our own
Far-off   younger sister

2.

But by then it was impossible:
After the first operation

She had been given five years
At most, she told us,

She knew the enemy was coming,
She was ready

Having done her research   worrying it
As if it were raw meat

She drew up her papers   arranged
What she would leave to the children,

Angular, ginger-haired, she laughed

With tears in her eyes   laconic
As any sage in her belly

Hungrily she would read
All night on the tightrope

From one nervous cigarette to the next

But in case of the worst she collected herself,
Stored drastic caches of medicine,

In the morning we'd go for walks,

We'd talk about clothes   we agreed
On suicide as a right

For she was a lion of great power:

Asking and not asking
All the days we knew her

Passionate, excited   but still tentative
The hoarse voice called our names

With quick fingers ransacking
Religion, philosophy, science

She pored over the texts   brilliantly

Leaving whole paragraphs of illumination
On scraps of paper at our door

3.

And would not stay to be thanked.

Wrapping herself in a thin quilt
To keep warm

She told no one   of course
When it began to happen

She said it was a headache
Maybe she even believed it

She said it was the bed giving her a backache
She bought three new mattresses in one week

And we thought she was mad

As the sparks smouldered, the disease
Hidden from everyone sprouted

In the dry timbers of her brain

Suddenly she was shouting
Over the smallest things she fought

Or laughed   for no reason

The words in her mouth twisted
Turned inside out,

All at once she'd subside

Into the most desperate
Curiously awkward hugs

"Sweetheart," she called everyone   staggering
On the brittle pipes of her legs

Until, finally, they took her away
To a hospital in the north

For the flames had invaded the whole house
Before she knew it:

For all her preparations,
The papers drawn up, the pills

There was no strength left to do it,

The last time we saw her
In her jersey nightgown like a teenager

Woozy   dragging on a last cigarette

Having pushed us all away
With half-truths   we had to believe

Vaguely the white face waved
High in a window   behind smoke

4.

And down here at the end of the telephone
All we could do was rage

At the animal howls   the thin figure

Shrunk to child size   the convulsions
The shaved head   in the bonnet,

But now, slowly, we begin
Little by little to accept it

For she was a lion of great power:

Though time shreds her into sawdust,
Though the house next door disintegrates

Into bells clanging, into fire
In the blazing stables of her eyes,

Though we look at ourselves   lost
In the empty movie theater of the world,

In the books she left us   in the mirror

Still, on the other side of the wall
The hoarse voice calls our names

For she swore she would come back:

The worn sweaters she left us
Shyly, put their arms around us,

In death daring what life did not

Something reminds us, wrapped
In these rough fibers

If giving and taking are one

This circle that is ended
Is only half begun.

— for M. Cameron Grey

THE MOVING VAN

Is waiting outside, it is always waiting
Ominous, offstage, with the powerful motor running

In Chekhov it is the sound of the axe, nowadays
The computer says it is time to go, time to pack up,
On to the next act

At the cocktail party we cling to our friends
In the jaws of evening, in the apricot sheen of the sky

Over the polished floor in a shimmer of topaz
Each separate face is distinct, dearer

And dearer than ever as the sun goes down
In halos of dust motes we are ranked

Around the room like a choir of modern angels
All singing together, with the help of the wine and the martinis

Each face is a sunflower, flushed in the afterglow
And tilted curiously, every which way

Under the cover of gossip, chitchat, the tiny fingernails of wit
Each watches the other, even the most sour

Over the winey Greek olives,
Over the salty bones of the anchovies even the most sweet,
The ingénue warbles her swan song but keeps one eye out for the others

For why else have we come here, over the toasted rounds of bread
With the children underfoot, with the old bore in the corner?

Dipping into the paté, we keep stealing looks
At each new wrinkle, each new strand of gray hair

Even as each one of them, each sad sign of change
Slowly softens into dusk, as the final curtain hovers

Over the interminable monologues, the last-minute jokes,
Throat-clearings, fidgets, the little half-conscious sighs

We heave into the room like gloves, the invisible hooks of wrist watches
In between drinks, punctuating sentences to remind us

The moving van is still there, a workman removes the last chair,
The prompter urges us to hurry but we can't do it,

Though the dust covers are waiting, in the wings
We will never return to the capital, this play will never end

If we can help it, the host thinks we will never leave
And maybe we won't, standing on one foot

And then the other, it is so hard to say goodbye
Over and over we keep telling each other the story of our lives.

THE OWNER

"Except the Lord build the house…"
—PSALMS, CXXVII, i

The water is blue soup, transparent
In Mexico, in the warm springs

Where the pool hunkers below the road
Surrounded by hummingbirds and willow.

But even though it is a tourist attraction,
With misspelled signs tilted along the highway,

Most of the time the place is empty,

Utterly given over to the soft rustle
Of swallows against the water

Except that this afternoon there is a straw hat
Floating on the surface like a ship.

Underneath it a man wallows
Quietly, feeling the smooth bottom of the pool
With his toes

But nobody notices, neither the pigs
Snuffling around among rusty springs,
Brand-new mattresses piled up in the yard,

Nor the people above his head going by
Without a glance downward, shuffling in the dust

With their burros, dogs, rickety buses like paintings
Silhouetted against the sky…

Even the Sunday paper, abandoned on the edge
Flutters its pages idly, there is no sound

Among the half-finished bedrooms the day lilies
Leap from the walls like tongues

Though the owner is never there
When we are, though it seems he detests children

The primitive kitchen is efficient,
The frying pan is still hot,

And the steps to the pool were just painted,
Its tranquil skin glistens

Clean as a blue teardrop

As the man moves his arms and legs
Swollen like a fat bug

He sighs, he sighs deeply:

Is the place being built up or down?
The silence does not say

But full of intoxicated bees dozing
Among their quiet skirts

All over the garden there are red roses,
Rows of them, with their dark faces

Carefully cultivated, flourishing
Breath sweet as tea...

Who takes care of them?

The man shifts his weight,
Loses track of a thought.

Nearby on the new grass
An old plastic hose coils
Just about to crack.

The owner, widely reputed to be mad,
May have big plans for his establishment
Or he may not.

THE MEANING OF LIFE

Even after a whole week full of it
Flapping,

Leather shoelaces
Untied

Those stormy petrels
My feelings

Refuse to settle down.

Friends come and then go,
Strangers take their place, or enemies...

What tempests
In a small town!

In the jammed daytime traffic

The whole switchboard's ganged up
On itself.

Has anyone got a boat?
I would sail out of all this

And you, too.

All these *explanations*
Poisoning the air like strychnine.

The doctor says one thing,
The professor says another.

I am beginning to see holes
Bigger than people, beckoning.

Each has his own story.

Sticking up in the air
Like the chewed skeletons of fish

The toothpick poles of masts
Sway around my bed,

But everywhere I go I am stalled.

Hands clutch at me like anchors
Begging me to stay still

And you want me to tell you the meaning of life!

In the middle of the night it crosses my mind like a yacht,
A pirate's lantern flickering.

I keep seeing it like a philosopher's raised eyebrow,

A firefly on a dark lawn
There where I'm struggling, huddled with all the others

The face of someone I love waving at me
One moment and then gone.

Finally she hardly even sees her best friend turn into a sofa,
Her next-door neighbor into a padded shoulder.

Fathoms farther down
She moves like an underwater grotto

Sluggish, swollen with years
Of easy living.

This is what comes of drowning
In love's arms.

The gift givers stand in the doorway

And she believes them, she accepts
Everything, everything...

She knows she has never returned anything,
Never had to respond

With anything but an aspirin or a pillow

But if she is as beautiful as a sea cow
What is there to criticize?

Before she knows it they have swum off,
Leaving behind them a cloud

Of inky kisses.

Sticking up out of the upholstery
Like rusty springs, like eyes

She feels them looking at her
And poking at her, sometimes, and she cries.

Stumbling from one dead chair to the next
She wishes she had picked them up,

Paid more attention to their smiles.

Now, drifting slowly past her
Belly upwards like fish

In the gloom she thinks she sees them,
Iceboxes, broken-down mattresses

With cotton batting bubbles
Streaming from their open mouths.

She lurches on her bed
And cries out after them, agonized

But all she really knows is water

And she's dissolving in it,
With the fluid rising in her chest

As the red liquid of her closets
Dribbles onto the sand

The feeble muscles flop
For lack of exercise, useless

And limp as flounders undulating
At the dim bottom of the world

With rivers for legs, with slow
Inland oceans for arms

She is a warped bureau, sodden
And odorous as an old rug

As the dry reasonable light fades
Above her, as every distinguishing feature blurs

All she can hear is a few sunken stones
Knocking together like prisoners

Signaling each other, far off.

The two pianos of their past are a pair of ravens
Each with the shiny black wings of an iceberg.

Settled in the living room they melt

Infinitely slowly, little rivulets of tears trickle
Like sad lullabies down their sides ...

Everywhere there's a dark throbbing.

Hollow, like the terrified breast
Of a seagull

Trapped, trying to get out

Even when they're silent
The sounding boards go right on protesting

But this is the center of the house, remember?

Dominating the concert hall
The giant portraits of our parents

Insist we go on playing for them

For each of us has a piano on his back
And sits in front of one forever.

With eyes like the polished depths
Of mahogany

The man looks at his wife over the black
Glistening humpback of a whale,

The woman sights along the lifted ridge
Of an open flying fish to see her husband

Full of overtones, the gold strings
Tangled like candy, like smooth satin

Valentines under the raised lids ...

But even when they take bows together
At every anniversary accept, modestly

The applause they both deserve,

At night, in the bedroom
Each hears the other's quick breathing

Crouched behind gleaming muscles
And bright blood

They chew up the pages of the present
Greedily, separated from each other

By their own music

From a great distance they wave to each other
Riding their loud animals

Through caves of hammers descending

Each keeps his own time, together, with the upper
And lower halves of the keyboards their parents left them.

THE MAN IN THE WETSUIT

The man in the wetsuit is here again
Dripping water and sloshing

As suddenly as the sea swallowed him

In black leggings, in black goggles and flippers
Clumping into the room

Horrible, his breath is mudflats
The color of pure logic, his two eyes

Roll in their sockets like horses,

Clownish, he scratches his beard
Brandishing a few dead fish on a spear

As if it were a victory but of what?
O friend I wish I could forget,

Once more you have returned
With an explanation for everything.

I would remember you calm
The way I left you, cheerful

Objective classifier of life

But here it is late afternoon, it is midnight
In enormous planks of lead

The sky comes down, there is no end
To the swollen chest you have grown,

O friend I thought I had forgotten,
Though it was your knowledge I chose

Out of all those others, ransacking
The cold chambers of the ocean

Though you taught me to name the sea
And swim in it, safe as a whale

Now, in the bedroom, foolish
Waving your slippery catch around

Though I hold out my hand, shivering
All over again at the slimy touch

Suddenly they fly away!

Over my head there are gargoyles grinning
That refuse to stay still, like the rest of the world

They refuse to be labeled, however sadly

In black plastic, a toy walrus,
You keep trying and trying

But the reproaches you breathe like the gas
Of a black rubber hose hissing

Are not mine, are only a formula

For whatever sweeps us away
At cross purposes, beneath our feet

Nameless tailfins flashing
In the darkness that surrounds us all

Strange currents, powerful
Feelings you would not accept,

O friend I wish I could forget.

THE REAL STORY

The news sweeps in like a blizzard
That staggers everyone

Like teeth grinding, heavy breathing

At suppertime, on the town telephone
As the wires between the houses churn

And writhe at the roots,
The school principal and the mayor

In cahoots! Oh God, what about the wife
And children? The song the littlest one sang

At the church picnic replays itself, stuttering
Into our stunned ears

As families split up into scissors

And everyone has at everyone,
All the old scores

Ride out like motorcycles to be settled
Once and for all, everything's mixed up with everything!

Secrets slip, private opinion
Red-faced, snipes openly from the newspaper

As half-truths take over the whole town.
At the nineteenth hole, at the bridge game

Slander comes flying like vomit,
Hardly an honest cup of soup, not one swallow

Of the cold milk of goodness is remembered or stays down
As long as we keep beating it, the dead horse

We dragged onto the golf course ourselves,

Whose clear outline disappears
Under the hard driving snow of our tongues

Into a large, gray-sided hill
That is covered with spittle like blood

And almost unrecognizable, by now

For the mayor and the principal have vanished long ago,
In the wild rubble of rumor their corpses barely twitch,

Though the children stand around staring
Like puppies, nudging at the cold flanks

We refuse to answer them, instead
We keep shouting at each other across town,

Like raw nerves in an open mouth

Pulling and tugging, exploring
Each individual possibility,

Whatever is worst about everyone,
Whatever least excitement

Is farthest from the truth,
In the pits of hysteria the hole,

The real story that is waiting for us
Hidden out there in the snow.

BIG TOP

The cathedral sticks up out of the gray mountain
Like the raw knuckles of a fist at the end of an arm
Or, since this is Mexico, an emaciated elephant
At a circus.

Surrounded by soda pop and flies
Half of him is peeling pastels and crumbling graffiti
In scrambled egg scallops, with people buzzing

And dogs: dogs snarling and yapping at each other
As hunched groups of women on their knees
Inch across the courtyard beating themselves
With small bright-colored whips while their starved children leap,

Wizened jumping beans stumbling, stubbing their toes and squealing
Over the bare scrabble of blind dirt shouting and squabbling
Over the shallow mud puddles and the fleas.

Meanwhile the cracked loudspeakers blare,
Waves of electronic hymns like syrup
Pour over the chipped, awkwardly inclined heads
Of saints like exhausted acrobats looking down

On the merriment below: the cockfights, the black bullring,
Bleeding gladiators, piles of gawdy trinkets
And trashy outdoor vegetable stands huddled

In every epoch, on the outskirts of every church
Before the Spaniards or the Aztecs or even the Romans
Every altar has supported itself on willing heaps
Of scribbled parchment, grinning cabbagehead skulls

And this is no exception; the ritual continues
The same as always: with draggles of dancing dogs
And spangled angels drooping in the dust

In the hot, tarred-over parking lot
The rusty chariots of old Chevrolets pull up
Belching mama and papa, visitors from Mexico City
In high heels and cameras, agnostic as they come.

Wiping their windshields of the splattered bodies of the flock
Of yellow butterflies they drove through on the swarming highway
They proceed across the courtyard, the little ones spinning

Gay plastic pinwheels in their black slippers and white socks
Until they arrive at the top and look at the kneeling women,
Like a pack of cheerful monkeys watching sad monkeys
Both bunches are bewitched, trapped on either side of the bars

By the man they call the ringmaster, the glitter of his gold
Shining out of the darkness of a giant movie screen,
But even his papier-mâché, his twirling sequins are nothing

To the huge venerable hide and long memory
Of that patient elephant whose massive skin endures
Everything, on the edge of the cliff where he stands
The grizzled walls rise up, his windy shoulders

Are sheer, gray, indomitable, with a perilous walkway
Of bowed arches for columns of silent monks
Collared over the abyss, a narrow stone bridge

Which the visitors traverse carefully, timid in the footsteps of the past
And swept upwards, off balance, by gusts from the valley below
Finally to the other side, a platform on the church's chest
So to speak, broad anyway, where the children immediately unfold

Into the soft wings of cartwheels, while the grownups pause to look
Peacefully out over the valley as if they were sitting on a throne
Like well-fed midgets in the palm of an enormous Hand

Or on the solid back of the elephant raised up
For what, they may wonder. But feeling a little foolish

With their backs to the wall they look out over the whole world
And though they are tempted, trembling there on the edge

Usually they refuse to think about it, ignoring the hungry dogs,
The bent women, the tattered children, the priest,
Also the stunning towers behind them, the white and gold hopes

That raised them here on high
For it's all only a circus, they tell each other, it's nothing
But a vast sideshow, a play almost as unimportant to our real lives
As those gloriously green meadows below us rolling away:

Meanwhile their beautifully dressed children
Are whirling on the platform, dipping and gracefully swooping
Frail as paper kites in all innocence challenging the sky

Which can easily become dangerous, surely someone,
Some mother or father must see it, this circus is a ship
Striding through waves of space, though the curious dancer
Perched on the pachyderm's forehead, the faint figurehead

Far out in front is blurred, all along the stone sides
Plastered there like ashes, fish in breaking foam,
The bodies of a thousand black butterflies out of nowhere suddenly appear

Like tiny trapeze artists, brave athletes, unknowing,
They have pushed their small selves high high up
Perhaps for warmth, perhaps for a quick look at the sun
But then, exhausted, they flatten themselves to the walls

And cling there, trembling, velvet children folded,
Pinned to the gray sides of the church
Like strange beautiful emblems, a lost corps de ballet

Mounted here for everyone, these black lace mantillas
Delicate, powdery, etched by the unintelligible script
Of centuries before them, the brief tissue of lives
That spread their fragile skirts for a moment and then die.

First it was a handful of black coathangers
it looked like, stuck out
in a barbed wire corral
a few yards from the long, wandering
tar and gravel snake stretched
over the bare hills from one distant
ranch to another: MIRV
missile site, of course, my Indian
friend raised neutral eyebrows: miles down
under the coathangers two scared
boys at the controls buried
forty-eight hours before they'd see
daylight again.

Next it was the low cabin
my friend's mixed-blood French
great-grandfather built,
squat as a riverboat
up to its hips in gray stone
beside the creek bed, scrub oak,
alder, fireberry, ouzels
flittering over cold green
water rushing down the protected
narrow corridor from Canada:
mountain goats, elk, grizzlies
in their time passing
secretly down the cliffs, over
the snow peaks, the pine
forests, maybe even
the dusty track we drove in on.

Then it was the long ramble
we took, miles out over the dry
wheat-colored hills, gray
silver ground cover crumbling

like old lace, steel sky
overhead, in all that vast
paper light nothing anywhere
but air, in sandy gulches a few
grazing horses looked at us
gently, snorting a little by red
faint-tipped sumac, fat snowberries
dove-winged, almost white pieces
of clay, tan chunks
skittering, scabbed rusty lichen
past Guerney's Butte breathing
the brisk turpentine of sage
as suddenly Jim shouted, grabbed
my left arm and stopped me
just short of the round
break-a-leg hole yesterday's
looking-for-oil-well
prospectors left uncovered.

Next it was hiking back
up the canyon to the cabin
at evening, trees along the sides
in the gathering dark closer
and thicker every minute, snow
on Old Baldy shelved,
shining down the ravine
under a cranberry sky shifting
from violet to black corduroy lit
by one star hanging, the sound
of dogs barking: dogs barking?
No, it is geese, Jim points
just over the horizon, the staccato
invisible river of honks rises,
pours over our heads higher
and higher, a hundred
no, two hundred! disappearing
wild coughs, pained
longing-to-be-home cries,

and then it was Sunday morning,
heavy artillery
detonating down the gorge.
Low booms, cavernous
rumbles under our bunks
woke us, drove us
out onto the chill bank
bare of any print but ours
and passing animals, birds
nowhere to be seen,
only in the ravishing blue
and clear air a chopper
full of oil-and-ammunitions
experts banging across quiet
bony hills with their delicate
apocalyptic instruments dragging aloft
over the weathered slopes a bright

     orange survey balloon!
Out of the desert it appeared
in all its poster paint glow
like a huge Disneyland cumquat
or a giant beachball, coy
as any Howard Johnson's
oasis we love
like Mother, all 28 flavors
sherbet cold, congealed
into one tangerine sphere hanging
right up there in the sky
where we put it, the cameras
snapping their top-secret shots
of hidden faults, underground
cracks filled with fire
whatever form it takes, ourselves
here in this bleak dawn
trapped in the open, stunned
under the clicking triggers

in the glare of appetite, stand
with our mouths open, craning
straight up at the fat
pumpkin silent as gas
over our pinched faces
caught only for a moment staring
and then gone.

Is dead serious about this one, having rehearsed it for two weeks
They bring it right into the Oddfellows Meeting Hall.
Riding the backs of the Trojan Women
In Euripides' great wake they are swept up,

But the women of the chorus, in black stockings and kerchiefs,
Stand up bravely to it, shawled arms thrash
In a foam of hysterical voices shrieking,
Seaweed on the wet flanks of a whale,

For each town has its Cassandra who is a little crazy,
Wed to some mystery or other and therefore painfully sensitive,
Wiser than anyone but no one listens to her, these days the terror
Reaches its red claws into back ward and living room alike,

For each town has its Andromache who is too young,
With snub nose and children just out of school
Even she cannot escape it, from the bombed city she is led out
Weeping among the ambulances,

And each community has its tart, its magical false Helen
Or at least someone who looks like her, in all the makeup she can muster,
The gorgeous mask of whatever quick-witted lie will keep her alive
At least a little while longer, on the crest of the bloody wave,

That dolorous mountain of wooden ships and water
In whose memory the women bring us this huge gift horse,
This raging animal of a play no one dares look in the eye
For fear of what's hidden there:

Small ragdoll figures toppling over and over
From every skyscraper and battlement hurtling
Men and women both, mere gristle in the teeth of fate.
Out over the sea of the audience our numb faces

Are stunned as Andromache's, locked up there on the platform
Inside Euripides' machine the women sway and struggle
One foot at a time, up the surging ladder
Of grief piled on grief, strophe on antistrophe,

In every century the same, the master tightens the screws,
Heightens the gloss of each bitter scene
And strikes every key, each word rings out
Over our terrified heads like a brass trumpet,

For this gift is an accordion, the biggest and mightiest of all:
As the glittering lacquered box heaves in and out,
Sigh upon sigh, at the topmost pitch a child
Falls through midnight in his frantically pink skin,

As the anguished queen protests, the citizens in the chorus wail
Louder and louder, the warriors depart
Without a glance backwards, these captains of the world's death
Enslaved as they are enslavers, in a rain of willess atoms

Anonymity takes over utterly; as the flaming city falls
On this bare beach, in the drab pinewood hall
The Reading Club packs up to go; scripts, coffee cups, black stockings,
Husbands and wives pile into the waiting cars

Just as we expect, life picks up and goes on
But not art: crouched back there like a stalled stallion
Stuffed in its gorgeous music box is the one gift
That will not disappear but waits, but bides its time and waits

For the next time we open it, that magical false structure
Inside whose artifice is the lesson, buried alive,
Of the grim machinations of the beautiful that always lead us
To these eternally real lamentations, real sufferings, real cries.

II.

THIS MOMENT

Hands that have waved farewell
Meaning, we will meet again,

Cities I had thought lost forever
That have returned to me,

Sooner or later I will see them again, the mountains
The white coffee cup beside my plate

Steaming in the cold, as suddenly solid
As the most miraculous happening

In the whole world, it is a gift
That is given to everyone, yes

Everyone:
The patterns of our lives

Repeat themselves, like the old woman
Who keeps looking into your eyes from a window

Right next to the tracks as the train passes
On its way to forgotten farmhouses,

The strict pine trees of New Hampshire
Like night watchmen in the snow...

For me it was a small town in Mexico
Flamboyant, full of flowers

Lying on a hillside with the moon
And bittersweet stars in its hair

But for me also it was the one man
I did not recognize,

At every turning point in my life
Like a small pony he would be standing there

Like an armchair with a cello in it, or a brook
He kept beckoning to me like the sun

Or a coffee cup, full of warmth
Until I accepted him, so that now

In the thick snows of New Hampshire,
In the dry deserts of Mexico

Over and over I keep finding them
Rustling in the wind like leaves,

Like growth rings in the book of trees
Hands that have waved farewell,

Cities I had thought lost forever
That have returned to me.

THE STRUCTURES WE LOVE

1. The Journey Underground

As if there were nothing left anywhere
But used furniture, lawn chairs

Draped in white sheets

In Proserpine's territory, the darkness
Sinking into the cellar

Leather boots and shoes
Trample you like dirt

Into thick chocolate, speechless
Stumbling over forgotten selves

Without recognizing them,

Shuffling through dusty rooms
Full of faded velvet

Shadows slouch and heave
With enormous caves on their backs

Between every breath
The animal

Paces back and forth, hungrily
Urging you to the staircase,

Up out of here to the sky

But all your intentions, like stout rakes
Club you the minute you step on them,

Earth plugs itself like cork
Into your eyes, ears, nose

And then freezes,

Congealed in the womb of winter
Roots squeeze themselves around you

Like a brown paper package dumped
Into a trash barrel

Hope muffles itself, the child
With tiny bound footsteps must learn everything

All over again,

At two you remember you had temper tantrums
Listening to your intestines suck sand...

Must all projects founder
In the Dark?

Half your life, in dreams
With every exit barred

In the basement, behind the woodpile
Among the cobwebbed trowels

All you can hear is the sound of earth
Turning itself over.

2. *The Journey into the Fire*

And then you wake up

Under the surgeon's knife
Of the breakup.

Don't do it, says the sofa,
Stay put, says your childhood,

Whatever it is, dullness
Is at least the absence of pain...

But worms are gouging out your heart,
They are about to eat it

Unless you take action
At once

You will stay here forever, smothering

In the overstuffed pillows of a past
That is banked ashes already,

Though flames sweep across the sky
Like scarlet animals in the trees

Though Cerberus snarls
At the gate

Houses you built, homes
In a haze of scorched memories twist,

Alternatives sizzle around you
Like fangs leaping for your throat,

Jaws you must pry apart

And then walk through them, the hot coals
Stabbing at your feet like teeth...

But to stay would be to forfeit everything:
In the hiss of gas, on the operating table

In the kiln of suffering your skin
Slowly hardens, glazed

All the colors of earth but empty,
Agonized, brittle, thin...

3. The Journey Underwater

But sooner or later you fill up again,
The soft pores open

Drinking freedom like a pond
Slowly you drift to the bottom,

Your hair lengthens, flows,
Rivers of fish swim beside you

Though words bubble and blur

Like shadows moving, voices
Outside your mother's body,

From inside, you hear them talking:

Deep piled as a rug
Warmth envelops you in a sheath

In every direction your roots stretch,
Reach up to the surface,

Your fingers separate like lilies
Swaying in the living room,

With your heart fluttering on your sleeve
You shake everyone's hand, smiling

With tears salting your eyes

For the risen phœnix is a waterbird,
Dear and clumsy as a duck

Like a willow washing itself in the ocean,
Like a nursing whale you relax

Sunning yourself on the surface, baptized

By pain out of hibernation, drenched
In the sopping wet feathers of luck,

Even in the midst of sorrow

You embrace everything, in the loose
Watery cathedral of the world

Kicking up your heels, and rolling

Paddling through it with your large flippers
Like a dolphin with its flukes unfurled.

4. The Journey into the Air

But even fish must be ready

For the last journey you will ever take
You think, preparing yourself ahead

For pitiless time going by
Like a feather

You will not feel, being split

Into flying molecules divided
And scattered everywhere

As flesh shrivels, in the wind
The juices evaporate, your joints

Cripple you in your bed
Faceless, flat out on the desert

Anonymous puffs of dust whirl
And plume erratically upwards

What's worst is the emptiness

Out there on the horizon

Green succulents, shade trees,
The ghosts of forgotten oases

Still hover in your mind, whispering
Whose hand will you touch, and how

If space is bodiless, with no eyes

What's left in the whole world
To comfort anyone

Except, in the labyrinth, a thread
Barely visible, the shadow

Of what we most hope is beckoning,
In the mythical kingdom of the bloodstream

In dreams the structures we love
Repeat themselves, like dim giants circling

The dowser's wand, that trembles
Between heaven and earth

And if we take hold of it, carefully
Hairsbreadth, a wispy particle

Rustling in the damp lungs of a cloud
At the far end of it may murmur

Whatever is dispersed gathers

Even as a storm gathers, as lightning
Shocks fiery life

Into dead hearts, on the operating table
The smallest piece of dirt in the air

Moistens, moistens
And swells

Globes circles drops
Spoonfuls of water gush

Pouring over the land
Heavier and heavier, coming down

And soaking into the cellar,
Among the dark furniture

The hairy brown bulbs
With tiny white eyes watching

And stirring everywhere.

THE ARRIVAL OF THE EGRETS

Suppose peonies, fifteen of them, white
Blooming in deepest winter among somber fir trees,

Relaxed, sitting on their large nests
Like huge heaps of fresh laundry in the branches

Shining back at us in the morning

From enormous clumps, mountains almost
Of snow

That has fallen overnight!

So the arrival of the egrets
In Mexico, when we were least expecting them.

Breathless, with hearts pounding
We raced to the roof to see them

And though they will soon sail away
Now, sitting on their nests like clouds

Just touching the tops of the Himalayas
On long elegant legs they teeter

And yearn upwards,
The white question marks of their necks

Fold and unfold themselves, the smooth arms of dancers
With the mild gaze of giraffes graze the heavens,
Patiently the young ones wait

For the parents to land, with a great shaking and fluttering
Each morning and evening

High up and then down, sweeping the air

The giant castle walls of their wings
Lift themselves over our heads

Into such beautiful plumed gardens

We can't help it, on tiptoe
Something is happening to us, not feathers exactly,

But balanced on the palm of an updraft
The spirit straightens itself, soaring

Until we are able to see them
As we are meant to:

With the smoke of sunrise in our eyes

Fifteen white candles,
Fifteen white exclamation marks standing

Against the dawn sky.

THE ODOR OF SANCTITY

Is like cookies, of course, oatmeal
Or plain vanilla on the blue windowsills of a childhood

That is never lost, but certainly not to this man
With his broad hay wagon shoulders, his huge wrists,
His jug ears like new cream,

With his fine handsome face smelling of spring floods
And the triumphant ozone of blizzards

He waves to us, a football coach
Solicitous as a cat licking its kittens,

When he puts an arm around you it's a bear hug,
Rough-tongued but milky

And salty too, like dried sweat it is strong
As wild clover, goose fat, charcoal

Or walnuts. Or ripe peaches
Or rich pipe smoke at evening
By a fire, with socks dangling...

Also it is delirious, after any excitement
It soars upwards, the wild whiff of hops
Mixes itself with juniper, over the city's breweries

But living out there by himself, keeping the sharp sting
Of his solitary labors hidden, constantly studying

Mostly he is alone, in the secret amber of the hive
Droning mysteriously, in tongues

Except that sometimes he will speak to us like a child
Simply, in his dark man's voice
Suddenly he will be crying out WHY?

With the clash of weapons, with agony everywhere
In every sewer bombarded, wracked, battered
The twisted bones of the poor

Like slivered onions, sour pickles
Piercing us with starvation's blood stench

In great pain he's as passionate as wet trees
Tossing their clear sweet gum at the storm,

In self-hatred he barks furiously at himself
Restlessly striding back and forth
Over the black harrowed earth like a hurricane,

But usually he keeps to himself, like a cloved orange
Shut up in a bureau drawer with all the spikes turned inwards
In the effort of silent prayer

Except for a few rare moments, when everything comes together,
When the blessed oil with its spice
Spills over the long sheets of his loneliness,

When the body kicks off its thick boots and leaps
With the scent of Easter lilies, outwards into the air

Far back in his eyes there will come a light,
The fragrance of candles, especially when he comes to call

With the slim envelope of his soul flapping
Over his head, the first clumsy biplane bumbling

In great friendly gusts, rich winey bucketfuls of hot tar
All the old cracked roads in the country heal themselves

Under the weather of his influence, like red apples in root cellars,
Cool rainwater on dry bricks
Among the dampening leaves at long last laying the dust.

— for Lou Catching

THE EGRETS AGAIN

In the pyramids of the evergreens
In the morning

The shock of them is the brisk slap
Of ice in a cold wash basin.

Brilliant in the treetops
Over the gray land

Blind igloos, eyes
Puffs of white smoke...

The miracle rings like iron.

Last night, just when I thought everything
Was lost

All fifteen of them came flying back,
Swooping in from the lake...

If only everyone could see them!

Calm eyeslits, periscopes
Drowsily stare at the sky

But these fat pearls
Have such long feet

Flexible as wire they reach
Upwards, pulling at my arms,

Preening themselves, magnificent
Feathers folding and unfolding

Lifting themselves into the horizon
Almost they take me with them

But not quite, not until you come with me

I'm stuck at the window
Trembling like a fool at the sight

My quivering spine
Might as well be a mast

For a whole clippership of birds

Swinging up into the one
Single transparent flap

Of heaven, high above land

Knocking like a boat in the bright breeze
At the fence around your yard

Over the desolate mine fields,
The bleak trenches of day

I'm crazy for you to come up here
And watch them with me,

Marvelous, in the distance
Cruising in from the mountains

Fifteen World War II bombers finally making it
Back to the home field.

SOME SAY IT IS CHRIST'S KISS

The bony curve of each back
Cradles its dark partner;

Half moons facing each other, slices
Of smooth yellow melon.

Bent protectively, brooding
Low to the ground as potatoes,

Gold seeds in the center
Of the hidden heart of the pumpkin,

We heave against each other in waves
Or hunker down, quiet as roses.

Some say it is Christ's kiss, the candle
Behind everyone's eyes,

That sinking into a cloud
Of thick red flesh
Inside the nubbed rind, the nakedness

Seamless, our round elbows
And taut buttocks fall
Into the hushed pond of evening;

That even in city bedrooms, sophisticated
As the cold clasp of diamonds

Over drowned skyscrapers
Love leaps in our bones, dancing
Shadows on the wall;

That the stars we make cluster
And curl into the wet core,

The bright orange pulp swirls
Into tiny solar systems, suns;

That the full moons of our parents
Long since have been swallowed up
Like children in the mouths of subways,

But that still in these groined vaults
A few embers remain

For breathing on, for flaring
Sudden as street lamps at dusk

Across the patterned grid
Of looming tall buildings

Thousands of tiny windows light up
Over our heads in a breastplate

Of small golden oblongs, chinks
In the black armor of night.

THIS MAN
(WHO WANTS TO FORGET THE NIGHTMARE)

This man who can blow smoke rings like a kite
Swooping over the bed, who is two pillows

Or four or five, or a field of poppies, or ten fingers,
Chinese firecrackers in the morning,

This man who is the two halves of a walnut
Opening out into a waterfall

This man who is pure muscle, a silk shirt
Rippling like the aurora borealis

This man who expands
From pleasure to pleasure like laughing gas

This man will confess anything,
Comforting businessmen, and drunks

With his arms around lonely women
This man who is spontaneous

Hotblooded, eager to do battle
This man who is a lift home

On a rainy day, a clap on the back, a big handkerchief
In time

Because what he wants most is to forget the nightmare
Of everyone's growing up

This man who was mugged once
Listening to other people's problems

On street corners, helping out beggars
Promising what he can't deliver

This man who wants to be a hero,
A brave regiment, a banner

This man is a geranium,
Blooming like happiness on the kitchen sink,

This man is a wool overcoat
For wrapping up pain, for putting it to sleep

This man who is wide-open, deep-chested, a trunk
Overflowing with old costumes, successful ideas, mistakes

This man who is bottomless, a still pond
Under a gray sky

This man will offer everything he has to everyone
Who passes by.

— for Leonard Robinson

GREEN HARBOR

I waited for you on the beach
Where the ocean liners passed by

Over the horizon and left me
Their cruel smokestacks.

Foam shuffled at my feet,

Impatient sandpipers skittered
Back and forth in their neat wedges

Fifty-two playing cards all turned
One way

I thought no one would ever meet me
Climb my solitary tower

I thought I would be cast away
On an empty coconut shell bobbing

Then you came riding
The one rail of morning

You whispered in my ear
My dear

Where you are going I'm coming
With you don't worry

Don't think of them the liners
Pass by and carry us with them

Foam-flowers in their wake

You know I would never leave you:
Now I have leapt the sun

My body is a rope of rubies
Fish heading straight for shore

Now the grotto is filled
Almost to the top

It is a clear pail
Of silver champagne we swim

Two seahorses suspended

Now I am a fan of light
A girl combing her hair

In the green falling a tree
Trembles in the wind, a harp

Bent to its knees and moaning
Down to its ankles my braids undone

Curl over the waist of the waves

Now as you fold me
Now as you spread me out

Hearts and diamonds in whole necklaces

The single note of a loon
Wails me down the stone steps

To where you are waiting, to a world
I drown in and then rise

With open fists palm upwards
To your face now mine;

In a charm of emeralds drifting
Back and forth in the harbor

For a little while it is certain the sea
All around us means no harm, no harm.

THIS MOMENT

And even after twenty years
It is as if we were the cool wax of leaves.

The smooth bag of your body
Is satin, neat as a boy...

If we were two swans we could not be
Swimming more beautifully.

Out on this patio, dancing
Under the placid radiance of the moon

The waters of the night draw back
And make a circle around us,

But under the soft lapping of the waves
An owl cries on the mountain,

Nearer there is a rustle,
The shifting of children's feet

And I cry out for them,
Myself, long gone, and you

Our pinched noses pressed
Against the glass wall of the world...

If only it were possible to go back,
Throw them a crust of the dream,

If only it were possible to tell them
Look! Everything came out all right...

But the loud noises of the party rise
Like a tinkling xylophone and fall

Like crickets wheezing, in the grass
This evening is ending, ahead of us
This moment is already past.

SUMMER SOLSTICE
(6/21/81)

All morning on the screen porch
I have been trying to live up to it.

Soon the weight of it will begin,
The drag of water against walking

But just barely:

Fifty years breathing seem to have blown away
Like pieces of milkweed, tiny stars receding

In a soft, unnameable drift
Of gray fuzz.

Are the days getting longer
Without me?

I know there are traps ahead

But I am too lightheaded to care,
Too absent to be brought down.

Years ago, when you came,
You lifted me out of a dark growling,

You tore me out of winter
Almost entirely.

Now, seated among the loose nets of the trees
Up here on my porch

A cold gust rattles the frames.

I know there are storms coming:
The fabric is starting to rip.

I know there are starved bellies
And armies of chaos out there, and eyes

Crying out to be filled,

But this is my world to walk in
Too:

For a little while, dissolved in it,
You and the wind hold my hand.

How fortunate I have been!

Far ahead of me the trembling
Transparent green galaxies of the leaves.

ACROSS THE WATER

The bird of music pokes holes in air

And we listen to them, distinct
Steppingstones across the water

Where the skin of the earth is stretched tight
Often it lets go, in ripples of fine gauze

The ordinary takes off its mask

Whenever I lie down for a minute
And stop talking, and listen

As from a sickbed I see you

Swathed in unaccustomed silence
And separated from myself, it is so strange

In a gold pouring of sunlight

Each wrinkle is a green valley, each bald spot
The triumphant bare crown of a mountain,

High overhead a jet rumbles its tin lid
But all around it, in soft bubbles

Sound shapes itself as sight:

Limned in blinding light,
Layers of transparent embroidery shimmer

With the intricate running and walking stitches

Of bands practicing, football signals
Babies, screen doors slamming

Outside our windows the whole town
Expands before us like silk

As the ice cream wagon comes tinkling,
Tossing its tiny pebbles

And everything in the room stops!

Each particle is familiar, each plain face
Magnified by the threat of absence

All that we love appears

Articulate as each leaf
On the tree of the large passenger liner

That is always hovering, across the water
At the outermost edge of the harbor

Filled with the throb of orchestras,
Sad dance music, clouds of departing wings

In the present that is always leaving us
Suddenly everything becomes clear

As one or two low voices speaking
Directly, in our ears.

III.

ENTERING THE GARDEN

Though there is no hand to push it,
No human being near,

The door heaves open, a chest
In the slow, horizontal impulse

Of household air coming in

And then going out again,
Mowing the dust of the threshold

With the barely perceptible creak
Of tiny, irritable crickets

Weeds in the cracks underfoot
Lift up their heads for a moment, the tips

Fray at the edges after each ponderous brush

And then bow down again, whispering
Under the blunt scythe of the arc,

And though there is no house around it,
No frame, no walls, no roof

The entrance and exit are real:
Memories of feet coming in

Or going out, on the worn sill
Slivers of old paint,

Faint signatures of lives
Almost finished, gone through

But still preserved, on the other side

With the soft haymows of childhood, hot tar,
Stickball on city streets...
As if the world were all window

From the non-chimney there is no smoke,
Like rays of light through the pupils

Birds plummet through the openings

And whether we are awake or asleep
Makes no difference,

Whether it is the shy embrace of a friend
Halting itself, in mid-air

Or whether it is a bright stranger

Winged, wearing a red baseball cap
Slouches against the doorjamb,

Morning and night they keep coming:
Seagulls, barn swallows swoop

From every hillside like breath
Over the non-doorstep

Sometimes even a stray dog, or a child
Or a truck, rumbling over back roads,

All that is other comes

As the secret leaves of the lungs open,
Then close, then open again, idly

Under the distant fingers of the sun.

You thought you were only going on a picnic but you aren't,
There is more to it than that.

Sitting here waiting for your friends

Somewhere in the center is a cracked voice
Gradually opening its mouth, and growing

For the young tree you are leaning against is moving:

Right through your backbone you can feel the smooth pole of it
Lurch back and forth, like a ship at sea that walks

High in the mountains, where the wind ruffles itself into whitecaps
And your hair lifts like feathers!

You know the crumbling dirt you are sitting on is a deck,
Inside the round hull of your body there are wings

There are compasses, strong spars
And a nose sharp as a prow to cut the wind

That is always with us, heavily moving through space

Especially at evening, in the blazing surf of sunset,
The slow heaving underfoot

You know you will have to set out anyway,
With or without your friends,

Crescents of Canada geese in their slim wedges
Swoop over the tall mastpole of your head

The black wall of the mountains stands straight up
In front of your face but there is another light

Behind it, always behind, the glittering bronze rim of it,
The vast eye of the universe like a lake

That is staring at you, mysterious, green at the far edges.

In the middle of the worst sickness yet
Most of the time you slept.

Flung on the bed like a loose skein of yarn

You were as patient as an old dog stretched out
On the back seat of a car in a parking lot.

No books. No TV. Occasionally I'd read to you,
But very little: perhaps we'd mention friends

Or hold hands, as if we'd never quarreled.

With starched nurses for fenceposts,
With intravenous tubes for lifelines,

Slow, slow, the pale serum dropped
Infinitesimally from above.

They told us you were getting better,
But three times, in the night

Gray-faced, your teeth yellowed and clacked.

Shaking the bed, delirious
You clutched the hot water bottle till it burned you.

Even so, even so.

The more terror banged at the door
The more we clung to each other.

Outside I suppose things went on
As usual: I was too worried to notice.

Chewing my fingers, making lists

89

How to Get an Ambulance,
Airplane Tickets, How Much...

Inside, after the nurses left
We'd ask each other, "Was that right?"

I was always rushing to the main desk to check
And then hurrying back to you, to rest.

For if we were planted in that room we were growing.

Breathing in and out
Quietly, quietly,

Even in the midst of it we knew
What else is there to do?

Exhausted, with the stunned faces
Of gaunt Indian cattle we browsed

Over the bare fields of earth.

The smooth walls reflected
A kind of gray, feathery light,

But entering the calm lake of that room
On tiptoe, careful not to disturb you,

Always the lurching gyroscope of my life tilted
And then settled,

Swaying slightly, with your breath

At the center of the world we lay peacefully
As birds in a nest.

For the odd thing about it is that often there is no noise
Or practically none, at the scene of the accident

The town fire alarm just stops!

And the victims are speechless,
Having done everything they could,

The crowd stands around waiting,

In deep grass cows stare
At the overturned car, still quivering,

After the roar of sirens, the fume
And boil of anxiety we emerge

Into this soundlessness as if it were a small glider

Where we sit motionless, in our ears
Only the soft sough of air,

Only a confused gratefulness in our heads
Like overgrown chrysanthemums to be pruned,

Once more cut down, snipped off,
All that is unnecessary thrown away

Into this white silence like the silence
Of incubators, the wrinkled flesh of birth,

Here in this room where we are both held
In some incredible suspension

Cloud-soft, beyond time drifting
On the lap of earth.

We are separated   almost at once
    From every airport we are calling

As the wash of liquid heat
    Disperses itself   love

Thins out, cooling
    Over the whole globe,

But after the first embrace
    In Sacramento there will be one pocket,
        Here and there others,

A few cooking fires   friends
    That still remain to us   flickering
        Just over the lip of earth,

Gathered around the hearth signaling
    Greetings from nowhere
        Touchable...

As the messages come back, jittering
    Over the torn wires

Lying in bed, I listen
    To the tapes they send, spoken

Days past: the children
    Fly back and forth, believers

They grow tomatoes, bread
    Rises   in small ovens,

Thread knots itself into islands
    Clusters of people waving

For the lacework of our lives
　　Is so fragile, by day

From East to West fingertips
　　Ravel, reach for each other...

But talking all night like candles
　　In the windows of the young

Though we gutter out by morning
　　In Mexico, China, Greece,
　　　　Each face cannot be present

Every minute　　where are you
　　Though the fabric rots　　the pain

Holds us together　　here
　　In Cuba, Alaska, New Zealand

Fire shoots across the heavens,
　　Or falls in the water, stunned

Tongues speak, burning
　　Chunks of meteorites whose absence

Is not absence　　in this life waking
　　In darkness　　I hear your voices

We who are one body
　　We who are one body.

IMPRINTS OF MICROSCOPIC LIFE
FOUND IN ARCTIC STONES

Blood splatters itself on snow:
Scarlet pomegranate seeds wink.

Out there in the white swamps, in barren fields of eyes

Hunger rackets through the air. Battered Chinese
Bleak pagodas, long blue centipedes.

Armies of anonymity advance,

But still there are flowers growing: magenta shreds on the peachstone,
Pink turnips in the root cellar.

Louder than jets I sing

For every miniature fossil locked
Motionless, in the old bones

But not vanquished, never:

With the small blood booming in our ears
It is always time to stand up,

In the farthest forests listen:

Bushes scratch at the stars, even the mole
Has velvet skin, and never goes too far.

Deceived by twitches and greed

Where there are too many leaders too many will be trampled
But either extreme is wrong, we are not helpless,

Neither have we any power but what we are given is ours

In fierce showers from the sun, in the vicious blast of a windstorm
Each particle rises, hordes upon hordes suspended

In the fine sting of blizzards forty degrees below zero

At the North Pole as at the South Pole each atom is alive
And fighting for it:

Though we are not heroes we contain all

Memory and the frozen memory of memory:
Neither are we stones but there are microscopic codes

In icy rock hidden, at each end of the world
In a dream of mastodons beyond all measurement breathing.

All over the forest the trees suddenly lift up
In faint protest, fluttering
As drops fall, jeweled delicate thimblefuls
From the flat green pond lilies of the leaves,

Shelf upon shelf of them, frail
Trembling along the air,
For the souls of everyone who has ever lived may still be here,
Who knows, there are silences everywhere

And we're walking among them, musing on our lives
Like numb flounders, one-sided because it is necessary,
Swimming among pine-covered mountains
As if there were nothing to be afraid of,

No nightmare about to fall on us
And pull out our eyelashes, flay the scales
From our dreaming backs, burn the last shreds of rope
From our hands.

For a while anyway we are safe, we think,
Surrounded by granite boulders like whales,
Scattered gray herds of them humping up out of the meadows
As if to nudge us aside but no,

We make use of everything, we sit on them for picnics,
On the Fourth of July we read poetry
And remember Neruda, buried among giant torches
Ignited for the last time,

The great lines tossed back and forth
And flaming, over the heads of jailers
Who can imprison no one, always there is one thing more,
One thing invisible that is moving

Between the wild strawberries there is a drift
Of such sweetness the mind almost swoons
And why shouldn't it, where do mushrooms come from
Overnight, small red dinner plates along the path,

What are these rivulets of coolness,
Trickles of fragrant cold brushing our cheeks,
Whose huge South American breath is that,
Rushing up from the Andes like an enormous brook

Full of salt mines and snow, of seagulls like confetti flying
And embracing everything – snails, politics, death
On every street corner but with such shouts of laughter
And such armfuls of passion we are spread out

Like spider webs, further and further reaching
The long lines stretch
Around the world, the spores of the spirit spurt up
Like insects out of tall grass,

Sap seeping through the tangled branches of the family
Of everyone we ever knew or did not know,
Millions of teen-aged guerrillas, children strewn on the roads,
Grandparents, husbands and wives, maybe even dictators

Who knows, maybe there are as many siftings of evil
As there are flecks of virtue, piecemeal on the forest floor
In the appalling undergrowth maybe everything is still shining,
Surging up through the shoulder blades of the ground

And out through the iron fists of the trees
With the green nosegays of the leaves,
Faint stars rippling, from their dark limbs stuttering
Among the invisible voices of the birds still fluting and calling.

What called to me from it was, when it arrived,
flat as a stomach in its smooth
brown paper envelope with the new poems, travel
announcements of other journeys, what

called to me from the neat grid of gray
typewriter strokes dense as the clean fibers
of an outdoor/indoor rug, the nap close woven, pre-
cise, industrious as ants walking together
in supple single-minded columns from

all directions at once raising up like true
and enormous saints a cathedral
that spoke to me, that grabbed my heart
like a rose and flew away with it,

murmuring the fine complicated texture
of the pure and impure: poetry as the wild
passionately lonely bridge between what is
and what we most desperately and forever

long for; "What a romantic!" my friend said, but she's
in favor of romance, only the night before,
at a talk I'd given about the particular, the letter
of the law, if it were really possible in art to use
the private to commandeer the general, out of the loose

amiable array of closed, individually shut selves
and meaningless pieces of time to create
those blazing battalions of abstract beauty
that *can* openly bloom in the church blade
even of only a single hieroglyph, she said

"But it's *all* opening and closing, isn't it? The chromosomes
rhythmically bend and twist
in and out like arms, like long ribboned braids," stooping
to tie her sneakers, the next day she wondered

"What's he like?" waving the part of the letter
I'd just given her to read before we left for tennis
as usual: out on the wide, eroded, bare
windy plateau at the foot of the patchwork mountain

with tin shacks, radio jingles blaring,
ricocheting from the canyons
on the other side: the lush green of the club, palm trees
like jewels, luxurious bougainvillea
and, right in the middle of the tennis court,

large wet puddles my friend, small, black-haired,
with snub nose and liquid muscles leaped over
quick as a goat but far more sinuous
and silkily graceful but tough, tough as a little
brown nut, how lucky she is, I thought,

the other part of the letter said diabetes
just discovered, don't worry, exercise
will help, but this one does it for fun,
though she has two children, paints, not much money
and sometimes the charming nose twitches

nervously, the tanned skin drains,
still she charges the net, growling, picking up
pollen from everywhere, dust, seeds out of the wind,
if she hits one she hits them all, she is one

smart woman, I know you'd like her, would know her
for what she is, swinging the tennis racquet wide
open and then swiftly, with great generous force closing
on the ball only to send it springing

round as a little moon spinning
in and out like petals, like the compact
closing and opening single
white athletic leaves of your letter.

THE NINE TRIBES

Among the broken fingernails of the ruins
Like middle-aged children, released
This once from our sticky skins

Lighthearted as paper kites trailing
Binoculars and jelly sandwiches

Halfway up the mountain we stand
With the dry breezes whipping through our bones.

Fifteen miles out there's another gentle swelling
Lined up opposite our own:

From the flat chest of the plateau a pale daytime nipple,
Our sister pyramid the moon pushes itself up

But here it is high noon:
The sky rests itself on our shoulders,

The broad sea of the valley stretches
In every direction like an airport.

In the grassy courtyard of the Royal Palace
A few glistening black bulls graze:

They shine at us like policemen
As we thread carefully among them
Our pasty white complexions from the Bronx.

Now no one is here but ourselves
And a few geologists, scratching in the ball court;

Otherwise the ants have it,
And the goats

But the guide is iron-lunged, jigging
On nimble caprylic feet,

He keeps chattering about his son Juan the archæologist
And then about the Nine Tribes

Who paused here once, in their thousands of miles trek
Down from soundless Siberia,

Who turned this hillside into a glittering citadel
And then moved on.

Now, lifted on a high platform of honey
History holds us in its arms

Light as lamb's wool, a shawl
Under the floating roof of the sky

As the folds of the present loosen, swell
And swoon outwards, like a silk tent
Under the gold breath of the sun

In the heat, in the sleepy drone
And cracked Morse code of the bees
The guide beckons mysteriously

And we wonder at it, the blazing
Small trumpet flower in his hand

But we agree to proceed anyway,
With arms around each other

Muttering American, that strange tongue
Slowly we follow him, panting
In the dry sweet dust

Up among the loose pebbles
And huge stones hacked
Into giant steps for the gods.

Then, almost at the top
In the windowless quarters of the priests

The maze angles in on itself,
In the stone jaws of the labyrinth
With the heat hitting us like a hammer

Suddenly I'm lost, I can't stand it,
EsMiss EsMoore in Mexico now,
Struggling to escape

I feel the guide looking at me, I watch
The ancient insinuations of his buttocks,

The hot fingers of the sun tangle themselves
Like claws in my loose hair,
And near the altar I know what he wants,

I stand there looking at him, dazed
By the brute fist of time

I think I believe him, almost,
That there is nothing in the world but flesh
And the sons and daughters of flesh

Lost forever, caught
Over and over again between the two nipples
On either side of the horizon,

As the sun and the moon rise up
Horribly, over the reedy chant,
The ritual leer of the guide's voice

For one second my eyes roll,
Blinded, I start to dissolve
Into the arms of the past

But still beside me I have you
Talking to me, and he has his work to do

On the long marches of the mountain we laugh
And shake our heads to clear them,

In the crumbling pyramid of this poem
We move on.

— for Betsy and Bob Fajans-Zimmerman

Many times I have seen innocence asleep
Beside me in the calm bedroom,

In the smoothness of white buttocks, the two pads
Of a water lily spread out on the sheets.

How fresh it is, how exciting,
On the verge of a new country, on vacation

With sprays of flame-colored bougainvillea,
With corn roasting, cactus blossoms, the bright sparks

Of coffee beans drifting across the mesa,

The tender embroidery of the breath
Weaves in and out, my eyes open

On such sweetness, the morning filled with air,

Outside our windows the whole of Latin America
Stretches itself to its full length,

With oceans on either side, bays, lighthouses, cliffs,
The narrow beaches of conquerors,

And suddenly I'm nauseated,
Boiling in hot sweat, angry

Thinking about hunger with its cracked feet,
Its blood pouring from the body

Where most of us can't see it, at the waist
In Central America the fountain

Spurts from the steps of the cathedrals
In waterfalls of young students, torn shirts,

Bullet holes and mouths gaping

Everywhere, even in this classroom
Here where I stand, behind the lectern raving

That it's all useless, everyone's too old,
Too selfish to do anything...

But then Gloria speaks to me, Gloria Dávila from Texas

In worn blue jeans, with her light voice
Quiet and earnest as an ant.

She'd much rather go back to the white bread,
To the ice cream of the United States,

But over the ancient land bridge,
Underneath everything she hears them,

The small feet of her ancestors shuffling
Like water trickling, thousands of tiny streams

Nourishing an entire continent...

And she won't let herself go back,
At least not for a while,

She wants to do translations, she is young,
In the bare libraries abstract as a nun

She pulls dictionaries around her,
In the toothpick boat of her pencil she sets forth

On the rough surfaces of the song
Of all the poets of Latin America,

That great mocha-colored river like a crocodile
Invisible as molasses, the slow jaws twining

Around our hips with the flashing
Of silver scales, the crushing weight of snakes

Shouting from the treetops like the brass trumpets,
The tattered bands of the poor...

For the rags of such language are a banner
Full of parrots and wild flames,

The hands of history beckon
From every bedroom,

The sigh of oppression is a wreath of buzzards
Knowing their time will come, revolving

In slow, voluptuous circles turning
Implacable as an alarm clock going off

In the white heart of everyone,
Even innocence, waking

To the red steel mills and the green orchids
Of Latin America, of work and Gloria waiting.

THE ENTIRE CATCH

— for Richard Hugo

Flopped on the bed, in the sodden overshoe flap
Of a large heart pounding, grown too big for its chest cavity,
Below scabbed hillsides he scowls but still wallows
In gold pools of beer, in the shallows of downtown bars
Hunched over shadowy counters he casts his long lines
Warily, warily, embraces the failed slug
Each of us knows himself to be, in jagged riffs of pain
That is pure cutthroat, moody, scathing, extravagant
But never sentimental: rain gargles comfortably in the gutters

For this is no laziness but a slow, serious settling
Into the true, the voluminous shape of a man mountain
At home wherever he is, at typewriter or baseball diamond
Slumped on the sidelines, in the inlets the sly ears wag
Like fins, the gills breathe naturally, feeding
On whatever passes by, rich sediment slipping downstream
From derelict ranches, railroad stations, small towns,
The outposts of all our lives crumbled into heavy silt
But picking up speed now, a distant waterfall whispers
Louder and louder, white lace speckles the brown

And suddenly he turns it, with a quick flick of the wrist
That is pure rainbow, in these rushing Montana
Clear streams of association the heart heals itself,
Tough as a pro football or a boiled egg
Quivering in its own tan jelly, a vague
Huge hunger to escape rumbles up from the boots
But the words come straight from the belt,
Buckling under to no colorless net
Of smooth nylon connections, fashionably pale polish

They leap straight up into the air, the spank
And wily slap of their tails sweeps up casual insects, seeds
Until there is no surface left, each facet

Churns into downdrafts, the blunt upturned logs
Of feelings he will not avoid rupture themselves and stand up
So skillfully in the rapids each twig of detail
Weaves itself to the other until the entire catch
Is raw, lyrical, unabashed, bleeding on bright gravel
And pulsing on the river bank, multiplying
From shadow into sunlight the subtle sheaves thrash.

THE INTERIOR MUSIC

Each morning a tune
      surfaces quietly,
            what is it, where

almost invisible, a bee
      drifting through fringed clover

threads itself through a drowsy needle:
      in the familiar fields
            of the head

the interior music, waking
      collects itself into small fluent eddies
            piled up against the fence of morning.

As sleep slowly winds down
      the heavy grooves keep turning
            languidly on the pillow

and what symphony has been conducting itself here
      or quartet, or jazz solo

why this particular piece
            of loose ribbon dangling

no one knows for certain,
      but picking it up, smoothing it

and then recognizing it, the pulse
            jolts to a startled halt:

over the body, that vague switchboard
      talking to itself

what strange calls have been made here
            in our absence?

All night long the connections
        keep humming and whirring

in dense octaves,
        layer upon layer in forkfuls,
                lean, many-turreted structures

playing all by themselves
        in the dark

inside everyone the music
        clicks its combinations and comes out
                here:

even when the plucked string
        is pure jingle, ridiculous
                as a dropped handkerchief

it feels like home:
        murmuring into its chest
                like a cello

the whole field lights up
        to the tips of the fingers

or falls on its knees
        in the rain

as the cobweb melody clings to us
        in long filmy strips,
                wisps of theme unraveled

all day it accompanies us
        like the two braceleted notes
                of a phœbe

plaintive in the late afternoons
        and then evenings, as if we had been printed
                with infinite horizons

stars imperceptibly move over the blackness
                    behind closed eyes

with the blurred after-images of planets,
                    tiny pinpointed spheres, glimpses

of entire systems breathing:
                    cadences, chords, harmonies

in flocks of precise dots,
                    whole echelons of information soaring

behind our backs:
                    over broad avenues and side streets,

out of stalled logjams, in sudden
                    shining cadenzas of spray

bridge after elegant bridge flings
                    its long lingering arch on air,

the sweet receding phrase
                    that keeps reminding us of the fine lines,
                              the barely visible network

that supports all bridges, once we have seen it
                    time after time

out of the darkness the quick flash
                    of the complicated gold harp strings
                              of the mind.

The sculpture is freeform, the young
woman making it large,
bulging beside black rock
sea-swirls, packed
granite chips she fits,
crams into the fluted folds

of hundreds of miniature
raw fragments, gritty shards,
pebbled gray chunks all pounded
together,
ground into this one
solid wave of stone reared up

out in the spring meadow frozen
but still flowing, shingled
shale and mica flecks graceful
as rivers
from her hands curving
grottos of midnight ice stopped

in its tracks! The smooth overhang
looms over her, fan-shaped,
almost falling but upright
in its place
as she in hers, stuffed
in tight dungarees tugging

so intimately at the round
marbled twenty-year-old
powerful hips and hearty
flesh winking
so sweetly at us
who can resist her? She works

patiently, sticking each new slab
onto the next, licking

strands of hair from her wet mouth,
pushing and
pulling, inch by inch
until it's done, precisely

the way she wants it, rough-surfaced
but slippery, the planes
sliding into each other
like oiled sheets
of matter moving
right out of itself, beyond

even the plump fists that shaped it.
Now through the hole she gouged
in the exact center we pass
in and out
like kids playing, charmed
but curious also, pulled

irresistibly through the archway,
the polished supple lips
smiling even as she smiles
to see us:
swimming through the sea's
ribbed caverns, the thick, vaulted

groined baptismal fonts of churches
could never be half so
exciting as this! Beauty
with such sly
gorgeous enticements
turns herself into an art-

piece so delicious we hardly see
what mesmerizing force
out of her own chubby, pink
openings
this statue starts up
in the bare seed beds all around.

The mind an eggplant in high heels! Yes
	The mind falling in love with music, with Venetian Doges
And Renaissance Princes, the mind mixing matzo dough,
	The mind taking elocution lessons and knitting,
The mind rushing through libraries like a hollow tube
	That sucks up everything,
The mind dazzling itself in the glass labyrinths
	Of Bach and Mozart, the mind soaring through the grand architecture
Of the Idea of History,
	The mind imagining everything has a beginning
If not a foreseeable end,
	Except music only chaos, clusters of random acts scattered
Like stars the mind pushes through
	With the narrow beam of a laser, the mind beginning to grow
Like a hungry snowplow that keeps heaping up
	More blackness each year, the mind having solved itself
As mere accident, after the destruction of history
	The mind insisting on its own limits, the mind knows what it knows,
The mind settles for trying to solve other people,
	Wishing to ignore telephone messages
And dentists' appointments, especially sad matrons
	Cooped up in their limousines, complaint after spoiled complaint,
The mind of a proud woman like a wasp's nest
	Trapped in its own digestive system,
The mind constantly going to the hospital with its family
	In despair, endlessly talking to the doctors
And then coming home to call the babysitter, make plans
	It knows it will have to keep, the mind familiar with bus schedules
And back stairs, with commercial toilets and townhouses
	The mind managing offices, hiring and firing secretaries
As often as necessary, the mind doesn't want to get its feet wet
	But the mind keeps right on greeting people and remembering them,
The mind skillful as a ticket-taker wielding a butter knife
	With plump flashing hands, the mind wearing purple
To set off its gray hair, the mind *hates* its own efficiency,
	The mind aware of its own shadows

And running from them, the mind wearing white gloves,
　　The mind wants to lose itself before Einstein
And then Palestrina, the clear distances of Vermeer,
　　Like a calm blinkered cow standing in its stall
The mind wants to watch the world go by
　　Without having to join it, how the mind suffers
The mind says to itself, but then takes itself to task
　　Like a mother, the mind powerful as an eggbeater
Dutifully goes on Peace Marches, watches election booths
　　And wipes noses, the mind can't help itself,
In the dark hive of the arteries all the bees are alive
　　Every minute, bursting like a ripe tomato
And ransacking every garbage pail and conversation
　　The mind races through laboratories and cathedrals,
The mind tries to control itself but it can't,
　　Even when it is cucumber-cool, an adult
Concealing itself behind crisp curtains
　　The mind never looks forward or back
With anything less than interest, a fat vegetable
　　To be prodded thoughtfully, to see what seeds it will bear,
Though the mind wants to give up everything
　　Especially as the veins harden, as all smooth surfaces wrinkle,
The mind thinks it has forgotten everything it ever knew
　　Even about lovemaking but it certainly hasn't,
Lying in the lap of the body
　　The mind does what it has to, the mind knows its own odors
And cold sweats, brooding into the ground
　　Like a tired watermelon the mind knows it will leave nothing behind
Of any substance but the mind remembers itself like a tower
　　With flights of doves beating in it, music it still hears
And will hear to the end, the absolute pitch rising
　　Out of the black earth of the garden, the brown body of a violin
Or a whole orchestra humming to itself, pouring over everything like the wind.

THE WIND OF OUR GOING:
ADAGIO MA NON TROPPO

Everything in motion!
　　　　　　　　No

Yes, it is
So, even in the blood

Cells veer and
Shift like minnows

Silver, swimming up
Stream and then down,

When I went out

For a short walk and came
Back home everything

Was gone!
　　　　　Soft sand

On a beach blows

From one day
To the next,
　　　　　　the grasses

Ripple and disappear

But come back
Again

We will smile,
Speak,
　　　　again

The passion

Of each atom,
If we should ever

Die, no!
            The heated

Wind of our going passes

Above us,
            into the trees

The irregular shadows
Fall

On a white wall,
                ribbons

Of a blown sand, fluid

Branches weave and
Flow, the wooden arms

Even of a chair have it,

The molecules heave but
Still change,

As on a bright October
Gusty day the yellow

Little oval leaves shower

Pieces of pure
Yellow glitter, even

When both of us
                are gone

In the slow movement

Of a Bach prelude, the ocean
On a gray day

Becalmed

Still the music pours,
The light

Yellow hooves
Of the harpsichord

Keep rippling and weaving

Over the cellos,
The dark

Machine of the universe,

The deep buzz
            of wood

In motion.

ENTERING THE GARDEN

As you are climbing the path between the two fields,
Threading your way upwards, among the yellow and red flowers,
You see her smiling, waving and urging you on

And suddenly you're afraid: entering the garden to be photographed,
Finally exposed, the secret of your true self
Revealed to everyone, nervous Narcissa caught

In the plain mirror of a sister's eye,
Of course you are uneasy: what if the camera should see
Something it should not see? Really, this is too naked

And too fast: the truth lies only *between* moments
Or so you say to yourself, holding your breath, listening to it
In the wet cave of the lungs hover, hesitate,

In stillnesses only you have experienced:
Nevertheless you agreed to this, you try
To appear comfortable, you arrange yourself and sit down

As naturally as possible, giving her your brightest smile
You stare back at your accomplice, the young woman crouched behind the tripod
With the black sheaf of her hair trailing its loose fingers

Over the high cheekbones and around the glass eye
Of the camera she hides behind, strange five-legged bird
Tap-tapping at the pale window of a day

You look anxiously out of, aware only of your own
Possible reflection in the smooth platter of the lens
Opposite you, the dazzling twin countenance

You would not disturb for anything, you wait to be shown
Not only yourself, but the world trapped in your mind's eye,
Imagining your own image in the concentric glass circles

Of the air that cages you, bewitched, sitting there like a lump
Still as a statue, unable to move
One inch for fear of losing the live face

You put on so carefully this morning, but what *is* this waxy trance,
This artificially still pallor? One slightest touch
Could utterly change the picture, could break you

And the camera too, into jittering jigsaw pieces,
And you know it, but this is not *nature morte*, the streaming
Coruscating surface of things moves constantly

And to catch it so must she, with her forehead like snow on the mountain,
Peacefully, draping her tall body nonchalantly
All over the camera like a bolt of fine cotton,

For though she is only human, though even those luminous cheeks
Can wrinkle themselves into the ugly crosshatches of the shadow
Of ordinary petulance, everyday cranky complaints,

Right now she is willowy, the white sail of her smile
Swoops out over her supple frame as if she were a mast
Leaning and bending with you, over a genial sea,

And little by little you let go, slowly you begin
Not quite forgetting yourself, but at least
Noticing other things, sunlight coming and going like minnows

Flickering over the sparse grass, the gawky arthritic sticks
Of flowering mesquite, the fringed pepper trees swaying,
The little pungent blossoms shivering,

Sprinkling the whole valley with their white spiciness
Until you begin to move too, to speak to her at last,
Even, cautiously, to look outside the garden,

And instantly the spell is broken, in a shimmer of crystal,
That spell that was of death, the dead center, the I,
Is shattered now, in a hundred leaping prisms,

Suddenly you look at the far mountains
With her, the camera begins to click
Faster and faster, tap-tapping at your head as if there were nobody at home

Which there probably isn't, but even if you have fled
Eerily, to the bottom of the next river,
What may not happen, from moment to moment,

In the swift current speckled, among the fragmented forms flowing
Through ribbons of light and shadow, matter in waves like water,
The entire tight knot of your being may splinter

Into a thousand tiny freckles scattered
Over the shaggy marigolds, twigs from the trees, nasturtiums,
Seeds in the air, your friend's feet, even the black ants on the ground,

So that now, finally, your held breath may relax,
Light as the chill breezes of morning coming and going
But painfully also, almost too transparent

And too excruciatingly fine for comfort,
Flashing in and out like the thin leaves of the pepper trees
Over the glass ladder of day, the scales that have fallen shining.

I have arrived here after taking many steps
Over the kitchen floors of friends and through their lives.

The dun-colored hills have been good to me
And the gold rivers.

I have loved chrysanthemums, and children:
I have been grandmother to some.

In one pocket I have hidden chocolates from you
And knives.

Speaking my real thoughts to no one

In bars and at lecterns I have told the truth
Fairly often, but hardly ever to myself.

I have not cried out against the crimes of my country

But I have protected myself, I have watched from a safe corner
The rape of mountains, the eagle's reckless plunge.

Ever since high school I have waved goodbye to history:

I have assisted you to grow
In all ways that were convenient to me.

What is a block vote against steam shovels?

My current events teacher was a fine man
But his moral precepts were a put-up job and I followed them.

Well-dressed, in my new Adidas
At every gathering I investigated my psyche with friends

And they investigated theirs with me.

But whenever Trouble came in the front door I ran out the back
And fell into the pit of my bones.

Escaped from those burning buildings, the past
What balance can any of us hope for?

I was comparing lipsticks
The day Nagasaki vanished.

The day Solzhenitsyn disappeared into the Gulag
I was attending a cocktail party.

Perhaps there are only ashes in my handbag.

A man at the corner of Broadway and Forty-Second Street
Tried to sweep me into a trash barrel and I almost agreed.

Already the dried blood was sifting along my wrists.

Already my own hands
Were tightening around my throat

But Sorrow saved me, Sorrow gave me an image
Of bombs like human tears watering the world's gardens.

How could I not answer?

Since then I have been planting words
In every windowbox, poking them to grow up.

What's God, that He should be mindful of me?

Sometimes I feel like wood
Waiting for someone to peel me.

Indeed I have been lukewarm
At heart, which is all that matters.

But I am afraid of disappearing
Into the wheat fields of a future

Of tiny bread colored atoms,
Equal fragments equally dispersed

That love each other and are never hungry.

What have I ever ignited
That warmed anyone?

I have not followed the rivers.

Dangerous as a pine needle
Packed in among others, in the dense multitudes

And dry timbers of the West

I am afraid of greed,
The rich taste of it, the anger

Hidden in my pockets.

Columns of smoke on the horizon,
Pillars of green fire.

But I have arrived here somehow,
Neither have I stopped talking.

Numberless are the kitchens I have sat in,
Chewing my fingers, trying to say something,

Anything, so that the daughters of men should see
As many sides of themselves as possible.

Word after word my footprints
Have stumbled across deserts.

How should I escape them?
They keep following after me.

A little wind stirs itself,
Whisks across my eyelids,

And I know what it is before I say it:

What if the world really articulates itself
In the socket of a human knee?

God save me
From the swamps of hubris but it may be, it may be.

Before the idea, the impulse.

I feel it moving in me, it is there
Arthritic but still powerful, a seizure

Delicate as grasshoppers, a light
Gathering in the skull.

Between thumb and forefinger
And the ballbearing joints of the tongue

In soft, glottal convulsions
Out of no alien skies

But out of the mind's muscle
The hieroglyph figures rise.

The little histories of words
Cannot be eaten.

I know it, you know it
And the children...

But the images we make are our own.

In the cool caves of the intellect
The twisted roots of them lead us

Backwards and then forwards.

If only we could understand
What's in our pockets is for everyone!

I have a dictionary in one hand, a mirror.

Strangers look at themselves in it,
Tracing the expressions they use

From one family to the next
They comfort themselves, murmuring

The tongues we speak are a blizzard
Of words like warm wool flying:

In the shy conjugal rites
Of verb, consonant, vowel,

In the dark mucosal flesh lining
The prismed underside of the skin

Each one is a spark sheared
From the veined fleece of the spirit

Of the looking-glass body we live in.

It is the one I have been cherishing,
The one all of us speak from,

For the world as we know it moves
Necessarily, by steps.

Breath, pulse beat, ten digital stops.

At the foot of the mountains I look up. Does God
Lift up His hand to cover them?

Blinded by tears like rain
My bones turn granite, the spine of the hills congeals them.

Where is the eye of the storm,
Or where is the center of my seeing?

The wind of my breath is a hurricane:
I am locked inside myself.

Painfully, up the bald stepladder I climb,

But sometimes the light in my head goes on
More like the sun than a match.

Just as they said in Arabia

There's a huge pantalooned angel swelling
Inside the body's glass jar.

The white-haired thread of steam
From the teakettle on the range whistles

And sharpens itself into a voice

Bodiless as history, invisible
But still whispering in ears

That keep trying to hear it.

It is as if midgets were bellowing their names
Down sets of cardboard cylinders.

But we have not disappeared
Yet.

My friends, we have said many things to each other

In new combinations, seed upon seed exploding
And blossoming in kitchen gardens.

I confess I am ashamed of myself:

I have not tried hard enough to understand
Or listen to you speak.

But the Word is mindful of itself
And always has been.

Littering every street

In the sly eyes of tin cans,
Drops of water in the gutter

The world looks back at us

From every known language:
Yoruba, Hebrew, Chinese,

Arrogant English, the subject
Subjecting all to its desires,

Even the softer tongues, romantic

Self-reflexive, done to
As we would be done by,

Whatever life we cultivate
Out of the animal moans of childhood

It is all wheat fields, all grass
Growing and being grown.

With poisoned bread in my pockets, or gumdrops,
Or armies like Myrmidons rising

What I say is true
For a time only, thank God,

If I have arrived anywhere it is to look
Carefully, at all I thought I knew.

In living rivers of speech
The reflections I make are my own

And yet not:

Though the old growth rings are hidden from us
And the echoing tomorrows of the acorn,

The warm currents of the senses
Are a two-way street, my friends:

The palms of our hands are crisscrossed
With as many intersections as a leaf.

EL DORADO

— for Elena and Bob Fleisher

By the side of the rented fishing boat he breaks
Up to the surface finally, out of the dark miles of the unknown

As if the godhead had been hooked at last!

And I gasp: not likely, not likely
But the water encasing him is so clear

The cold gray envelope is an eye
He's at the center of:

All forty-five pounds of him surge
Like a jeweled arm, a monster club flashing

Solid as a gold bullet, royal ingot of the ocean
We paid for ourselves, the raw mystery of it roaring

Silently after us, at the end of a nylon line

> *And that should be the end of it,*
> *The rainbow turned into a side of meat,*
> *The great fish into steaks*

But even as we haul in, in, as the wet sack
Of the stunned body's flung down on the floor

The huge haunch runs with paint!

Iridescent as sunrise
Streams of lavender, rose, salmon

Diamond eggs of color swoop
Back from the tail, in strawberry rivulets

That ribbon along the sides, the heaving satin of a world
That is changing before our eyes!

Each color bleeds into the next
As in the open wound of a trail blaze

The bubbles swell, blister,
And swerve into each other,

The apricot, the pink, the fresh orange of dawn
Wash over the cold flanks

In lustrous coppery swags that slide,

That droop downwards as the gleam fades,
Loops into matte, into dull bronze...

And still it goes on:

> *Though we shift uneasily in our seats*
> *On different buttocks, with new profiles*
> *And altered eyes we watch*

The green sparks of a thousand fireflies
Over the deep indigo, the gun barrel taut muscles

In the heat of daytime crackle:

Each freckled wing whisks
Over the side like rare mica

Or gathers into flares, into hot embers
Of red tongues that leap but then subside

Into brown, into steel, into thick ink
Into serge blue that is icy, almost black

Until it is finished, finally, we tell ourselves,
The dumb frozen body of this world

Will stop changing, stay put, give in
To what we know is waiting
Like fool's gold, at the end of the trail

But even as the helmet head stiffens,
As the eyes in their gilded spectacles glaze,

Veil after veil of pale azure sweeps over the carcass
Like wisps of cloud at sunset

They jet stream high over the skin
Striped, whipping across the sky

As if meteors were messengers, keys to unlock a city
Of promises we wish we could believe in:

Though the straight lines of their passage frazzle,

Almost instantly they clot
Into tiny moons, sapphire blue

Pinpoints on a gay canvas, a circus
Of celestial eyes winking

Until it is I who give up
Under my breath begging "Stop!"
What will never stop, even as the stars go out

At that moment the dorsal fin like a flag
Shoots up into the air and keeps right on changing

Valiant, ridiculous, the heraldic pennon
Jaunty as a last hand waving

In the one reflex that is left
Flying

PATRICIA GOEDICKE

A native New Englander, Patricia Goedicke has only recently returned to this country after fifteen years living and writing in Mexico. Winner of many awards and author of six previous volumes of poetry – her poems have been appearing in magazines like *Harper's*, *The New Yorker*, *The Nation*, and *Hudson Review* for some twenty-five years now – she currently teaches poetry in the Creative Writing Program of the University of Montana. She lives in Missoula, Montana, with her husband, the poet, short story writer, and novelist Leonard Wallace Robinson.